Discovering the Titanic

By Cindy Trumbore

Modern Curriculum Press

Credits:

Illustrations:11, 14, 16, 18, 25, 30, 32, 37, 40, 41, 47: Joe LeMonnier.

Photos:

Photos: Front & back cover: Emory Kristof/National Geographic Image Collection. Title page: Popperfoto/Archive Photos. 5: NTB/Ipol, Inc. 6: Ulster Folk & Transport Museum. 7: Ipol, Inc. 8: t. Popperfoto/Archive Photos; b. L'Illustration/Sygma. 9: Ulster Folk & Transport Museum. 10: Blank Archives/Archive Photos. 11: Ulster Folk & Transport Museum. 12, 13: Brown Brothers. 15: Ulster Folk & Transport Museum. 17: L'Illustration/Sygma. 18: New York Times Co./Archive Photos. 19: Delphine Star/Tony Stone Images. 20: Ipol, Inc. 21: L'Illustration/Sygma. 23: The Walter Lord Collection. 24: Ipol, Inc. 25: UPI/Corbis–Bettmann. 26: Popperfoto/Archive Photos. 27: AP/Wide World. 28: ©Hank Morgan/Photo Researchers, Inc. 29: AP/Wide World. 31: Diego Goldberg/Sygma. 32, 33, 34: Emory Kristof/National Geographic Image Collection. 35: AP/Wide World. 36: Emory Kristof/National Geographic Image Collection. 37: Archive Photos. 38: Reuters/Discovery Channel Online/Archive Photos. 39: Emory Kristof/National Geographic Image Collection. 41: t. AP/Wide World; m. Bruce Dale/National Geographic Image Collection. 43: Sygma. 44: l. Low Films International Inc./Sygma; r. Popperfoto/Archive Photos. 45: Popperfoto/Archive Photos. 46, 47: Ipol, Inc.

Cover and interior design by Agatha Jaspon

Pearson Learning Group

1-800-321-3106
www.pearsonlearning.com

Contents

For Dale, Mary-Kate, and Brianna,
my *Titanic* experts.

Chapter 1
Treasure Hunt

In August 1985, a ship called the *Knorr* set out to discover hidden treasure. On board was a man who was a scientist and a dreamer. His name was Dr. Robert Ballard.

Other people had tried and failed to find the treasure. It lay on the ocean floor, 2 $\frac{1}{2}$ miles under the water. There is no light that far down. There would be nothing to show Dr. Ballard where to go.

Dr. Ballard was not an ordinary treasure hunter. He was a well-trained geologist, a scientist who studies the earth.

Dr. Robert Ballard ▶

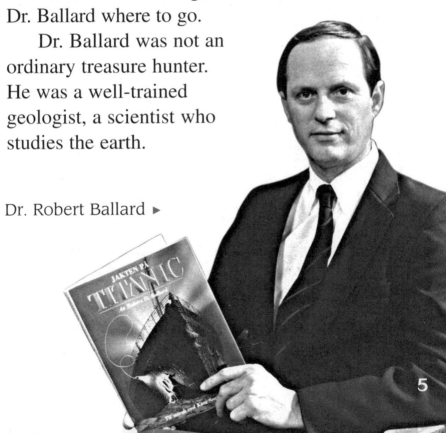

▲ Building the *Titanic*

Dr. Ballard had dreamed of making this trip since 1973. He spent 12 years getting together the money, the ship, and the machines that would help him in his search.

He also was not looking for ordinary treasure. His goal was to find the *Titanic*, a famous ship that had sunk 73 years before.

There were many stories and many mysteries about the sinking of the *Titanic*. Many years later, people were still fascinated by it.

When the *Titanic* set sail on April 10, 1912, it was the largest passenger ship ever built. It was named for the Titans, huge make-believe people who were once said to rule the earth.

Titanic was a good name for this ship. It was the largest movable object ever made— nearly 900 feet long and as tall as an 11-story building. The ship was longer than the Washington Monument is high. The steam from its 29 boilers rose from three huge funnels along the top. A fourth funnel was just for appearance.

▼ The ship about to sail in the movie *Titanic*

Inside, the *Titanic* was like a floating palace. It had its own Grand Staircase as well as a gym, elevators, and a swimming pool. There were two barber shops and a restaurant with 49 tables. Also on board were some very valuable things. One was a rare book covered with jewels. Another was an expensive car.

▼ The *Titanic's* gymnasium

▼ A bedroom on the *Titanic*

▲ The *Titanic* ready to sail

This was the *Titanic's* first voyage. It was set to sail from Southampton, England, to New York City in the United States. Traveling on the ship were 2,224 people. Some of them were the richest and most famous women and men in England and America.

The great ship was said to be unsinkable. Yet late on April 14, 1912, the *Titanic* hit an iceberg and began filling with water. About three hours later, it sank. Because there were not enough lifeboats to save everyone, 1,513 people lost their lives.

▲ Front page headlines

Many things were known about what happened to the *Titanic*, but there were still mysteries about the way the ship sank. Where was it, exactly, when it went down? Did the *Titanic* break in two as it sank, as some survivors had said? Was it lying in one piece at the bottom of the ocean? Was it possible to find any of the treasures that were on board? Were there any bodies still lying on the ocean floor?

Dr. Ballard was determined to find the answers to some of these questions. The sinking of the *Titanic* was one of the great tragedies of this century. The story of how the lost *Titanic* was found tells about one of the great discoveries of the century.

Legends of the *Titanic*

A novel written in 1898 predicted the fate of the *Titanic*. The book was called *Futility, or The Wreck of the Titan.* The author wrote a story about a British liner sailing from Southampton, England, to New York in April with 2,000 people aboard.

In the book, the *Titan* hit an iceberg and sank. Nearly everyone drowned. The reason for so many deaths was because there were not enough lifeboats.

INDIA INK

Chapter 2

The Voyage of the *Titanic*

◄ John Jacob Astor walking with his wife, Madeleine, and their dog, Kitty

The *Titanic's* passengers came from all walks of life. John Jacob Astor was the wealthiest man on board. A multi-millionaire, he was traveling with his wife and their dog.

Another wealthy passenger was Isidor Straus. He owned Macy's, the biggest department store in the world. He and his wife, Ida, were returning to the United States after a vacation.

There were also ordinary people on the ship, like the teachers and bankers in second class. The people in third class were mostly immigrants. They were hoping to make a new life in America. Then there were the crew members. Everyone from maids, to bakers, to "stokers" worked on the ship.

▼ Stokers like these people worked in the ship's boiler rooms shoveling coal.

Diagram of the *Titanic*

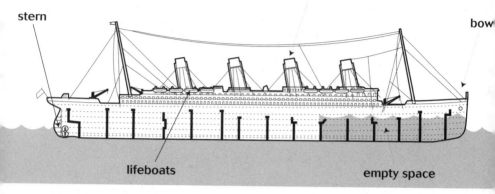

▲ Side view of the *Titanic* showing 16 empty spaces that were supposedly watertight

People could not imagine any accident that could sink the *Titanic*. It had 16 empty spaces in its bottom. Each space was said to be watertight. If one filled with water, its doors would close, trapping the water. The ship was made so that it would float if any two of those spaces were full of water. In fact, it would float even if the first four spaces were flooded. No one thought that could happen.

Thomas Andrews, one of the passengers, was sure the ship was safe. He was a director of the company that built the ship! J. Bruce Ismay was the head of the White Star Line, which owned the *Titanic*. He was on board, too.

The captain, Edward J. Smith, had worked for the White Star Line for over 30 years. He was looking forward to the end of the voyage. He planned to retire after the trip was over.

▼ Captain Smith inspecting the *Titanic* with a passenger

The first five days of the *Titanic's* voyage were very normal. The ship made stops at ports in France and Ireland to pick up passengers and mail. Then it sailed off across the Atlantic Ocean toward America. Captain Smith expected to reach New York on April 17. By the fourth day, the ship was already approaching Newfoundland, near Canada. Then came the fifth day, Sunday, April 14.

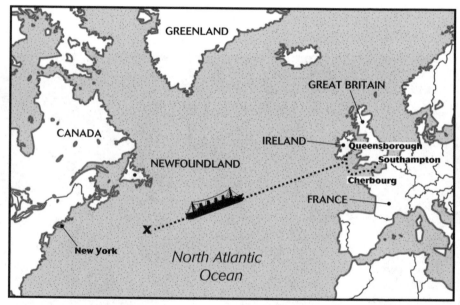

▲ *Titanic's* route from Southampton to where it sank

Wireless operator,
M.G. Phillips ▶

All that day,
the men working
in the wireless
room had been
getting messages
saying there were
icebergs in the
water ahead. The
wireless sent and
took telegraph
messages by radio.
The wireless room was
where the radio equipment
was kept. Wireless was still a new form of
communication in 1912. It was called wireless
because the messages traveled through the air
instead of through wires.

As the ice warnings came in, the wireless
operators sent them up to the bridge. This was
the room where the officers in charge ran the
ship. Captain Smith paid no attention to
these warnings.

▲ Captain Smith

It is hard to say why Captain Smith did nothing about the warnings. He knew that making a fast crossing was important to J. Bruce Ismay. Perhaps Captain Smith didn't want the ship to fall behind by slowing down. So, the *Titanic* traveled on at full speed.

Legends of the *Titanic*

Three brothers by the names of Alfred, Bertram, and Tom Slade had signed up to work on the *Titanic*. They were going to shovel coal. However, they were held up at a train crossing. All of them missed the boat. Because of the train, their lives were saved.

INDIA INK

Chapter 3
The Tragedy

Like all ships, the *Titanic* had a crow's nest. This was a platform high up on a pole. In the crow's nest two lookouts sat in the freezing air on the night of April 14. At 11:40 P.M., one of the lookouts saw an iceberg. He rang the ship's bell three times and picked up the telephone.

"Iceberg right ahead," he told the officer who answered. Orders were given to turn the ship. But the orders came too late. The *Titanic* hit the huge iceberg and soon stopped.

▼ An iceberg very much like the one that caused the *Titanic* to sink

The iceberg badly damaged the side of the ship. Water began to pour in. Captain Smith and Thomas Andrews went to look at the flooding. Five of the spaces meant to keep the ship afloat were quickly filling up with water. The men realized with horror that the great ship was going to sink in just a few hours.

At first the passengers did not believe anything was wrong. After the ship hit the iceberg, it seemed to be steady. Then it began to tilt or tip to one side. Captain Smith ordered his officers to begin loading the lifeboats.

▼ Lifeboats being lowered in the movie *Titanic*

▲ One of the lifeboats with people who were saved

The *Titanic* had 20 lifeboats, more than the law required. These boats could hold 1,178 people. However, there were over a thousand more people than that number on board.

The women and children were told to board first. There was so much confusion as people tried to get to the lifeboats that many of the boats left when they were only half full. Soon all of the lifeboats had been lowered to the water. Over a thousand men, women, and children had been left on board to die.

Some people chose to die bravely. Mrs. Straus was offered a space in the lifeboats. She said no. She did not want to leave her husband. John Jacob Astor did not get into a lifeboat. First, he put his wife in a boat. Then he went to free his dog from the kennels. He ended up going down with the sinking ship.

Other people were cowards. J. Bruce Ismay got into a lifeboat and left the ship, even though few men were being rescued. He said there were no other passengers waiting for that boat. Some people said he pushed his way through a crowd of men. For the rest of his life, people would whisper that he had acted badly.

At about 2:15 on the morning of April 15, the *Titanic* went down. The bow, or front part of the ship, sank first. As the bow sank, the lights went out in the ship. The back part, or stern, rose high up out of the water. There was a terrible roar as everything movable on the ship—furniture, dishes, pianos, and much more—slid forward. The hot boilers exploded when they hit the water.

Isidor and Ida Straus ►

23

People couldn't agree on what happened next. Some said the ship went down in one piece. Others said it broke in half between the third and the fourth funnels. Then the *Titanic* sank out of sight. That was the last anyone would see of the ship for 73 years.

At least 1,500 people drowned or froze to death in the icy waters of the Atlantic Ocean. The dead included John Jacob Astor and Captain Smith. The brave captain had chosen to go down with his ship.

A few people who were holding on to floating objects in the water were able to get into a boat. After several hours, the people in the boats were rescued by another ship called the *Carpathia*. Out of more than 2,000 people on the *Titanic*, there were only 711 survivors.

Titanic sinking bow first as seen in the movie ▼

Some people in the lifeboats were unusually brave. One was Margaret Brown. She took charge of rowing lifeboat Number Six. She also saved a man's life by wrapping him in her warm fur stole. She became known as "the unsinkable Molly Brown."

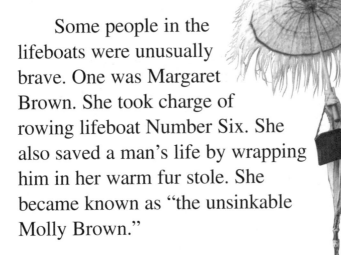

Molly Brown ▶

Legends of the *Titanic*

Only about one ninth of an iceberg can be seen above water. The men in the crow's nest had trouble seeing the iceberg for another reason. The pair of binoculars that belonged there had been lost.

INDIA INK

Chapter 4
The Dream of Finding the *Titanic*

For years, people dreamed of finding the *Titanic*. The waters in which the wreck lay did not belong to any country. Anyone could try to find it. However, nobody knew exactly where the wreck was.

People thought they knew. When the *Titanic* was sinking, the wireless operators had told all the nearby ships where it was. Nobody was sure, though, just how fast the ship had been going when it hit the iceberg. The sinking ship would also have drifted in the ocean currents.

▼ Wireless telegram showing the last message from the *Titanic*

▲ Dr. Ballard holding model of *Titanic*

In 1953, the first attempt was made to find the wreck of the *Titanic*. In late December, a ship from England searched for days in the area where the *Titanic* was supposed to have sunk. It went back in 1954. On neither of these tries did it find the *Titanic*.

In 1973, a young scientist by the name of Robert Ballard began to think about finding the *Titanic*. He was working in Woods Hole, Massachusetts, at a famous institute for studying the ocean.

Dr. Ballard was part of a team working with a submarine called *Alvin*. The sub could hold three people. It was built to go under the water to study the ocean. Until 1973, *Alvin* could not dive very deep. The pressure from very deep water would cave it in or crush its hull, or frame.

▲ Submarine called *Alvin* used to find the *Titanic*

Alvin was changed in 1973. A new kind of steel made its hull stronger. Now it could dive 13,000 feet, which is nearly 2 ½ miles. That was deep enough to reach the place where scientists thought the *Titanic* lay on the ocean floor.

For years, Robert Ballard tried to find people with money to help pay for a voyage with *Alvin* to find the *Titanic*. He had an idea about how to take pictures of the shipwreck. He planned for *Alvin* to pull an underwater sled that held lights and cameras.

The sled that Dr. Ballard developed was called *Angus*. *Angus* carried cameras that could make a map out of underwater pictures.

▼ Picture taken underwater by *Angus* of a lifeboat davit or holder

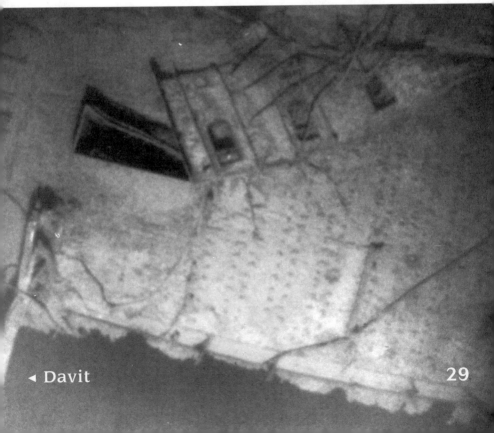

◄ Davit

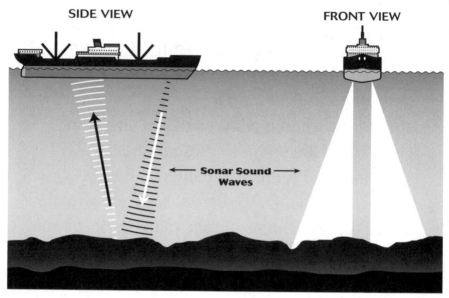

SIDE VIEW   FRONT VIEW

Sonar Sound →
← Waves

▲ Side-scan sonar mapping

Finally, Dr. Ballard was able to borrow a ship from Woods Hole to start looking for the *Titanic*. The ship used a sonar mapping system. The sonar bounced sound waves off any objects that lay to either of the ship's sides. Scientists could "read" those sound waves to find any objects that lay underwater.

Dr. Ballard left Woods Hole in his borrowed ship in 1977. However, the trip was cut short. A large drill pipe used to lower equipment into the ocean came loose and fell into the water. Valuable equipment was lost. The ship had to turn back.

Others took up the challenge of finding the *Titanic*. In 1980, a ship left Florida in search of the wreck. A Texas oilman named Jack Grimm was in charge. He hoped to find some of the lost valuables at the bottom of the ocean.

Grimm had looked for famous things before, such as Noah's Ark and the Loch Ness monster. He hadn't found them. To search for the *Titanic*, he hired scientists who were experts in using sonar in the deep ocean.

Grimm's search ship sailed back and forth in the area of the *Titanic's* last distress call. The sonar system on board covered one part of the ocean floor after another. Nothing was found.

◄ Jack Grimm

Grimm made another trip in 1981. This time his team had better equipment. They found something on the bottom that seemed to be a large

▲ Propeller

propeller. Grimm thought it might have been one of the three propellers that drove the *Titanic* forward.

Legends of the *Titanic*

The *Titanic* was hard to find for many reasons. It went down in very deep water. In the area where it sank is an undersea canyon that made it hard for sonar to find the ship. The position *Titanic* radioed to other ships when it hit the iceberg also wasn't the exact place where it went down.

INDIA INK

Chapter 5
"There's Something"

While Jack Grimm was searching the ocean, Dr. Ballard had been busy. He was working on a system he called *Argo*. *Argo* was a better model of the underwater sled than *Angus*. It had five video cameras and two sonar systems. One system looked to the sides and one looked ahead. This would allow the scientists on a search ship to take very fine pictures of the ocean floor.

▼ *Argo*

▲ Jean-Louis Michel *(center)* with Sar vehicle that has side-scan sonar

The U.S. Navy agreed to pay for a test of *Argo*. What better treasure to test it on than the *Titanic*?

In August 1985, Dr. Ballard set sail on the research ship *Knorr.* He led the voyage along with a French scientist, Jean-Louis Michel.

Before sailing, Dr. Ballard decided he would not look for the wreck. Instead, he would look for the debris field, or trail of objects that would have fallen from the sinking ship. He also would use *Argo's* video pictures instead of the sonar system to find the debris field.

The search team reached the place where they thought the *Titanic* had gone down. They pulled *Argo* back and forth, back and forth, over the ocean floor. *Argo* sent very detailed pictures up to the video screens on the *Knorr*. They showed a variety of undersea life and lots of mud. Dr. Ballard began to wonder whether he would ever find the *Titanic*. Was it lost forever?

◄ The research ship *Knorr*

▲ Jean-Louis Michel watches the video screens.

By the end of August, there were only a few days left for the *Knorr's* voyage. The ship had to turn back on September 5.

At midnight on August 31, Dr. Ballard took a break. Jean-Louis Michel sat in the control room with a few other crew members. They watched the screens, which showed pictures from *Argo's* five TV cameras.

Around 1:00 A.M. on September 1, one of the crew members said, "There's something." The cameras had picked up the trail of debris from the *Titanic*.

The crew called for Dr. Ballard. He ran to the control room. On the screen was a big piece of metal. Dr. Ballard knew they had found one of the *Titanic's* boilers. Everyone cheered. Then, before the searchers went to bed, they had a few minutes of silence to remember all the people who had died on the *Titanic*.

Legends of the Titanic

Some good came of the *Titanic's* sinking. After the disaster, countries joined to watch for icebergs at sea. New laws were also made for ships. More attention is now paid to ships' radio messages. Lifeboat drills are required. Perhaps most important, now there is space on a lifeboat for every passenger.

Chapter 6
A Mystery Is Solved

The next morning, Ballard and Michel sent *Argo* back to the debris field. Their equipment showed there was a big piece of the wreck nearby. On September 2, *Argo* went looking for it.

▼ Bow railing of the *Titanic*

▲ View of a tall pole called the mast that fell from the deck

Soon *Argo* came to a large, dark object. It had found the *Titanic's* bow, or front of the ship. Dr. Ballard could see the ship's boat deck. Now it was clear that a large part of the ship was in one piece, and standing upright. But was the whole ship there?

Argo's pictures of the back of the wreck soon showed that the stern, or back of the ship, was missing. The team found it lying 1,970 feet beyond the bow. Its decks had collapsed and it was facing in the other direction.

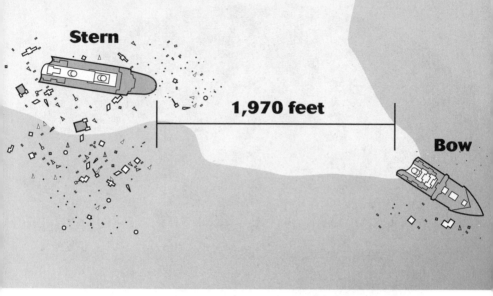

Stern

1,970 feet

Bow

▲ Map showing the distance between the bow and the stern as they were discovered on the ocean floor

This discovery proved that the *Titanic* split in half just before it sank. It broke between the third and fourth funnels because the ship's Grand Staircase made a space there. The bow part sank first. The stern seemed to settle on the water for a moment. Then it too sank. The people who thought the ship sank in one piece were watching only the stern go down. Dr. Ballard and his team had solved one of the mysteries of the *Titanic*.

The discovery of the wreck of the *Titanic* was reported all over the world.

When Dr. Ballard talked to the press, he spoke of how peacefully the wreck lay on the ocean floor. "May it forever remain that way," he said.

Unbroken dishes from the *Titanic* as they settled on the ocean floor ▶

Legends of the *Titanic*

The pocket watch shown here was found on the body of a man pulled from the water after the *Titanic* sank. The watch stopped just before 2 o'clock. The ship sank at 2:20 A.M.

Chapter 7
Return to the *Titanic*

Dr. Ballard returned to the wreck the next year, in 1986. This time he traveled to the wreck inside the submarine *Alvin*. He saw how the bow of the ship was buried in 60 feet of mud. Great needles of rust hung from the hull, or body, of the ship. Dr. Ballard called them "rusticles." He was sad to find that the ship's beautiful wood deck was gone. It had been eaten away by sea creatures.

▼ Two bollards on *Titanic's* deck were used for the lines that tied the ship to the dock.

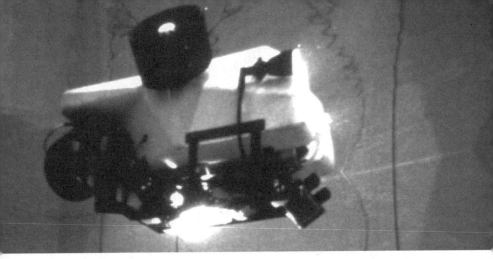

▲ Jason Junior

A robot called Jason Junior was part of the dive. With its lights and cameras, it could go into smaller areas than *Argo* could reach. Dr. Ballard's team sent Jason Junior inside the wreck. Its pictures showed lamps, pieces of machines from the gym, even the cranks used to lower the lifeboats.

The team had decided not to touch the wreckage. They thought that anyone who wanted to study the site should see it as it had been found.

To Dr. Ballard and his team, the *Titanic* was like a grave, although they did not find any bodies. But they found sad reminders of the tragedy. A doll's head lay on the ocean floor. A pair of shoes showed where one body had come to rest.

Other searchers did not share Dr. Ballard's feelings about leaving the wreck untouched. In 1987, a new team went to find the site. They took away 1,800 articles, including the ship's bell. They arranged a special program on TV to open a safe from the *Titanic*. The safe was empty.

That same team went back to the wreck in 1993 and 1994. Again they took thousands of objects. People flocked to see the pieces in a museum show. Some of the *Titanic's* survivors were angry that the wreck had been disturbed. Others were glad that the accident was still remembered by so many people.

▼ An unbroken cup lies on the ocean floor.

▲ This doll was found in the water after the ship sank.

When the *Titanic* was discovered, some tests were made to help people learn more about why the ship sank. One test showed that the steel used in the *Titanic's* hull was not very pure. In icy water, it could break. A few rivets, or metal screws, from the millions used to hold the hull together were also tested. They, too, were found to be of a poor grade of metal. They might have popped when the iceberg scraped along the hull.

Some people thought the wreck could be raised. In August 1996, a team tried to lift a part of the hull. The cable broke.

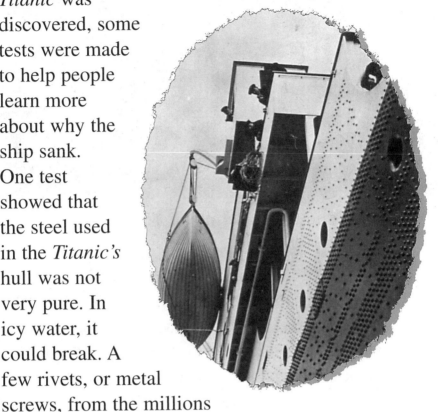
▼ Closeup of the hull showing the rivets

45

▲ A scene from the movie *Titanic*

In the 1990s, the story of the *Titanic* caught the fancy of movie director James Cameron. He decided to make a movie about the ship. To make his movie more true to life, he dove to the wreck in a small submarine. A swimming robot called *Snoop Dog* went inside the wreck to take pictures that Cameron used in his movie.

The movie was hard to make. For the ship, Cameron had a nearly full-size model built. He had to sink the model in thousands of gallons of seawater to make the movie as real as possible.

When *Titanic* opened in 1997, it quickly set box office records. In 1998, the movie won 11 Academy Awards, including Best Picture.

Our ideas about the *Titanic* will change as new discoveries are made. No matter what scientists learn, though, the *Titanic* will continue to fascinate us. It reminds us that people can be brave in the worst of disasters, and that nothing is truly "unsinkable."

James Cameron ▶

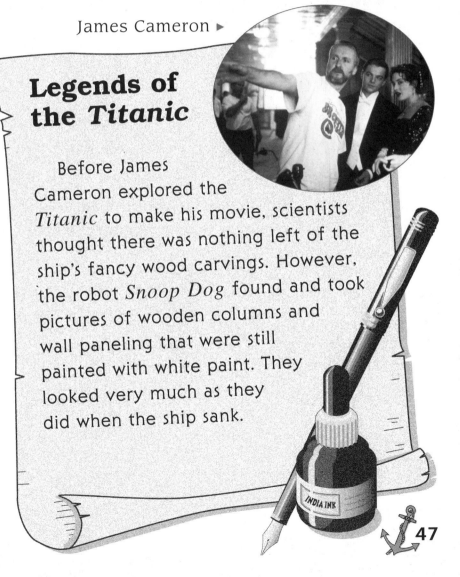

Legends of the *Titanic*

Before James Cameron explored the *Titanic* to make his movie, scientists thought there was nothing left of the ship's fancy wood carvings. However, the robot *Snoop Dog* found and took pictures of wooden columns and wall paneling that were still painted with white paint. They looked very much as they did when the ship sank.

INDIA INK

Glossary

binoculars (bih NAHK yuh lurz) a pair of small telescopes fastened together; used with both eyes to see things far away

boiler (BOIL ur) a tank in which water is heated to make steam for power

coward (KOW urd) a person who runs from danger or trouble

funnel (FUN ul) a smokestack on a steamship

iceberg (EYS burg) a huge mass of ice floating in the sea

immigrants (IHM uh grunts) people who move from their home country to a new home in another country

sonar (SOH nahr) an instrument that uses sound waves to find an object in deep water

telegraph (TEL uh graf) an instrument used to send coded messages over wire or by radio

tragedy (TRAJ uh dee) an event that is very sad

voyage (VOI ihj) a journey or trip taken by water